GRIN - Verlag für akademische Texte

Der GRIN Verlag mit Sitz in München hat sich seit der Gründung im Jahr 1998 auf die Veröffentlichung akademischer Texte spezialisiert.

Die Verlagswebseite www.grin.com ist für Studenten, Hochschullehrer und andere Akademiker die ideale Plattform, ihre Fachtexte, Studienarbeiten, Abschlussarbeiten oder Dissertationen einem breiten Publikum zu präsentieren.

Dokument Nr. V10925 aus dem GRIN Verlagsprogramm

Nadine Klemens

Girl Interrupted: Comparison of book and movie

Nadine Klemens

Girl Interrupted: Comparison of book and movie

GRIN Verlag

Bibliografische Information der Deutschen Nationalbibliothek: Die Deutsche Bibliothek verzeichnet diese Publikation in der Deutschen Nationalbibliografie; detaillierte bibliografische Daten sind im Internet über http://dnb.d-nb.de/ abrufbar.

1. Auflage 2002
Copyright © 2002 GRIN Verlag
http://www.grin.com/
Druck und Bindung: Books on Demand GmbH, Norderstedt Germany
ISBN 978-3-638-74660-1

Technische Universität Braunschweig
Englisches Seminar
SS 2002
HS Film and Literature

Girl Interrupted. A comparison of book and movie

Nadine Klemens
6. Semester

2

Contents

1. Introduction

"'You spent nearly two years in a loony bin! Why in the world were you there? I can't believe it!' Translation: If you're crazy, then I'm crazy, and I'm not, so the whole thing must have been a mistake (125)." How do we know whether someone is insane or sane? Susanna Kaysen's account <u>Girl, Interrupted</u> is told to us through the eyes of a girl who is diagnosed with a borderline personality disorder- can we believe the things she is telling us, or are her memories distorted by her mental illness?

The unreliability of the first-person-narrator is not only a question when dealing with the book, but it is also an interesting aspect to consider when taking a closer look at the cinematic version of <u>Girl, Interrupted</u>. In order to analyze how Kaysen's literary work was adapted, I will first shortly introduce the book and the movie. Then I will compare the two works with regard to narrative perspective, plot and time frame, characters, and cultural background.

2. The book

Susanna Kaysen's memoir <u>Girl, Interrupted</u>, first published in 1993, deals with her stay in a mental hospital in the late 1960s.

When sent to McLean Hospital after a suicide attempt by a psychiatrist she had never seen before, Susanna is torn out of her directionless life and finds herself in a mental institution. At the hospital, which is renowned for its famous patients, the doctors say she has a borderline personality disorder. Susanna feels as if she was put into a "parallel universe (5)" that is unconnected to the outer world. The shocking encounter with the other patients on the women's ward causes her to think about the nature of insanity, about her suicide attempt, and about the life she has been leading before coming to McLean. After 18 months, she is considered sane enough to go back to the outer world and become the wife of a boy she dated during her time at high school.

From the first-person-perspective, episodes that give a vivid impression of how life in a mental institution during the 1960s must have been like are juxtaposed with pieces of Susanna's original hospital file. In the episodes, Susanna depicts the daily routine and the hospital rules. The reader not only gets to know the other girls on the women's ward, but is also confronted with Susanna's philosophical thoughts concerning the nature of insanity, life, and

death. Each episode treats another aspect that is connected to the hospital, craziness, and the problems of the patients on the ward. The episodes are only loosely related and rather than following a chronological pattern, they constitute a trail of thoughts, a kind of inner monologue. However, chronology is achieved by means of the hospital documents in the book. They give the reader information and medical facts about Susanna, and one gains insight into the bureaucratic system surrounding her hospital stay. The documents are structured with regard to their date, starting with the case record sheet that is the first page in Susanna's file.

The book is thus focused on mental illness and the concerns, fears, and problems of a teenager on the way to adulthood. It is Susanna's story, told by her thirty years after her stay at McLean, hence, it is a reflection of a now grown-up woman who is not quite sure whether she is still crazy or not. She says that she is not even sure if she had ever been crazy. "What does borderline personality mean anyhow? It appears to be a way station between neurosis and psychosis: a fractured but not dissembled psyche. Though to quote my post-Melvin psychiatrist: 'It's what they call people whose lifestyles bother them.' He can say it because he's a doctor. If I said it, nobody would believe me (151)." What she tries to express with this is that the psychiatrist who sent her to McLean was disturbed by the youth of the late 60s, and that for this reason, she ended up in the hospital. "Take it from his point of view. It was 1967. Even in lives like his, professional lives lived out in the suburbs behind shrubbery, there was a strange undertow, a tug from the other world- the drifting, drugged-out, no-last-name youth universe- that knocked people off balance. One could call this 'threatening' to use his language (40)." In addition to this, she says that different kinds of mental illness are fashionable at certain times, and that in a few years, her illness would not be in the books anymore. Long after her stay at McLean, Susanna wants to know what exactly her diagnosis means. "An analyst I've known for years said, 'Freud and his circle thought most people were hysterics, then in the fifties it was psychoneurotics, and lately, everyone's a borderline personality.' When I went to the corner bookstore to look up my diagnosis in the *Manual*, it occurred to me that I might not find it in there anymore. They do get rid of things- homosexuality, for instance. Until recently, quite a few of my friends would have found themselves documented in that book along with me (152)." So the

definition of insanity seems to be closely linked to the society at the time of the diagnosis.

3. The movie

While the thematic emphasis in the book is put on Susanna and her borderline personality disorder, the cinematic version of <u>Girl, Interrupted</u> by James Mangold is more concerned with the actual events on the ward and the relationship between the girls. Susanna (Winona Ryder) and Lisa (Angelina Jolie) develop a friendship, or rather, Susanna develops a dependence to Lisa. After the first shock, she is impressed by Lisa's rebellious character and the freedom she expresses. "A suicide attempt lands her [Susanna] in Claymoore, a mental institution. She befriends the band of troubled women in her ward (Georgina the pathological liar, the sexually abused Daisy, the burn victim Polly), but falls under the hypnotic sway of Lisa, the wildest and most hardened of the bunch (imdb.com)." Besides the friendship of the girls, the movie also deals with the question whether Susanna will ever get out of the hospital. In this respect, Valerie (Whoopi Goldberg), the head nurse, influences Susanna the most. The two women develop a close relationship, and the talks with Valerie make Susanna realize that it is up to herself whether she will ever make it back to the outside world or become one of the long-term cases on the women's ward.

4. Plot and time frame

The movie tells Susanna's story chronologically, but Mangold works with many flashbacks and -forwards to tell past events. Furthermore, the plot has a closure as the establishing shot shows a scene that takes place after the showdown at the end of the movie. The closure of the movie establishes another time frame than the book does. In the book, the discourse time is 1993 and most of the story takes place back in 1967, so there are roughly 30 years in between. In the movie, discourse time and story time cannot be clearly distinguished, as we have a lot of flashbacks, and sometimes we do not know from which time the voice-over tells us the story. The establishing shot suggests that Susanna sits in the underground tunnels of the hospital and reflects upon her stay in the hospital. At the very end however, the voice-over says "most of us got out eventually", which conveys the impression that this is told to the audience from some time in the future.

Moreover, Mangold adds quite a bit to the original plot, and also leaves out most of the philosophical thoughts we find in the book, nevertheless, he sticks to the nucleus of the original plot. Some episodes of the book that tell about the life on the ward at McLean (which is called Claymoore in the movie) can only be found in details, as for example the episode "Checks", which describes the rule that patients have to be checked on by the nurses at regular intervals, or the episode called "Sharps", where Susanna explains why they are only allowed to shave their legs with a nurse watching. He changes some episodes in order to put a different emphasis, namely, to focus on the girls and their problems. He enhances Susanna's story with Georgina's, Polly's, and Lisa's story.

The most striking example of an episode that has been changed and lengthened is the story of the sexually abused Daisy. In the book, she is characterized as "[…] a seasonal event. She came before Thanksgiving and stayed through Christmas every year. Some years she came for her birthday in May as well (31)". The episode furthermore describes Daisy's addiction to chicken and laxatives, and the passion for the apartment her father bought her. It ends with the news of Daisy's suicide shortly after she had left the ward to live in this apartment. In the movie, however, the episode is lengthened and used to show how Susanna is drawn to Lisa. The two girls run away together and visit Daisy in her apartment. Lisa is mean to Daisy, making fun of her father and her addiction to chicken. They scream at each other until Daisy cries and goes upstairs. Susanna does nothing to help Daisy, and when she finally looks after her in the morning, she finds her dead body in the shower. While Lisa runs away, Susanna waits until the police and the ambulance arrive, and is taken back to Claymoore by her doctor, Melvin (Jeffrey Tambor). She feels guilty because she did not stand up against Lisa, but Valerie assures her that she would not have been able to prevent the suicide.

5. Point of view

The point-of-view character in both works is Susanna, although we find occasional shifts of perspective in the movie. The first-person perspective of the book is transformed with the help of cinematic techniques such as voice-over and subjective camera.

In the voice-over narration, Susanna reads out the thoughts and experiences she writes down in her notebook. The voice-over narration resembles the style of the narration in the book: it is Susanna's distanced view of the hospital. In the movie, the rather rational voice-over stands in contrast to the confusing flashbacks and –forwards that question the reliability of Susanna as the narrator. One passage in the book conveys the impression that Susanna is at all times aware what happens to her: "I wasn't simply going nuts, tumbling down a shaft to Wonderland. It was my misfortune- or salvation- to be at all times perfectly conscious of my misperceptions of reality. I never 'believed' anything I saw or thought I saw. Not only that, I correctly understood each new weird activity (40)." But how can you believe someone who says she lives in a parallel universe? How reliable are people who live in a mental institution? However, as the book is written 30 years after Susanna's stay at McLean, that is, at a point when the narrator's mental illness is recovered, we do believe her. Her thoughts about insanity appear to be highly rational, even intellectual. So the only aspects about the narration that the reader may doubt are Susanna's experiences in the hospital. In the movie, the ambivalence between reliability and unreliability, sanity and insanity is expressed by the rational and distanced voice-over narration, the thoughts in the notebook, and the confusing shifts between different levels of reality. With the help of the flashbacks and –forwards and subjective camera technique, the audience is taken into Susanna's mind. The fact that the audience does not know in which reality they are in takes up the questions about the narrator: if she does not know where she is and what she sees, how can we believe her? On the other hand, there are also reaction shots by an objective camera, that are used more and more towards the end of the movie. These shots express the recovery of Susanna's state of mind, hence, these shots, again, suggest that at least part of the story is true.

The first sequences of the movie are exemplary for the use of all these techniques. The establishing shot shows Susanna, Lisa, Georgina, Polly, thus, the main cast, in the basement tunnels of the hospital. A voice-over narrator introduces the audience to the movie: "Have you ever confused a dream with life? Or stolen something when you had the cash? Have you ever been blue? […] Maybe I was just crazy. Maybe it was the 60s. Or maybe I was just a girl-interrupted." Then, the camera closes in on Susanna and in a flashback we see

Susanna in the emergency room where her stomach is being pumped. The flashback is shown from a subjective camera perspective. The audience sees the things that happen in the emergency room through the same restricted and blurry view as Susanna does. Then, we get a reaction shot of her, showing how she mumbles incoherent things. After this, there is a flash to the doctor's office. The doctor interviews Susanna, but she is distracted by a dog barking outside. She associates this with a dog barking at her father's birthday party. The camera then closes in on Susanna and another flashback fades in, showing Susanna at the party through a subjective camera. The subjective perception of the event is emphasized by the muddle of voices that appear to be too loud, as the audience gets the feeling that all of this too much for Susanna. The doctor's voice slowly gets through this muddle and the action is back at the doctor's office. A reaction shot shows how Susanna is disturbed by the visions she has. Hence, a lot of events are told to us through Susanna's eyes, and the shifts of realities and the shaky subjective camera express her unstable psyche at the beginning of the story. Like her, we perceive different levels of realities and are not able to control in which reality we are in. As the movie procedes, we get less and less of these techniques, therefore, one can conclude that the stability of the camera signifies Susanna's state of mind. Thus, we get more and more reaction shots towards the end of the movie.

The majority of reaction shots throughout the movie show Susanna. Most of the remaining shots show Lisa, Georgina, Polly, Daisy, and Valerie. In this way, the main characters of the movie are clearly demarcated from the other women on the ward, whereas we do not find a group of main characters in the book. The shots appear to be taken by an objective camera, therefore, we tempt to believe the things about the other girls more easier than in the book, where their stories are told to us by Susanna. There are a lot of shots of Lisa, at some points in the movie one could even go as far as to say that she is a second protagonist.

An interesting shift in the point of view, executed by a reaction shot showing Polly, is when Polly watches Susanna and Tobias in the parking lot. The shot of her sad face and the emotional breakdown in the evening are details transformed from the episode "Fire." In this part of the book, Susanna realizes that she might get out of the hospital some day, but the burn victim Polly is "locked up forever in that body (19)."

6. Characters: description vs. cast

In the movie, there are not only changes concerning the plot, but also concerning the selection of characters. In the book, for example, Susanna does not even mention her parents, whereas in the movie, they play a bigger role. Here, they are used to give reasons as to why Susanna ended up in the hospital. They emphasize the image of Susanna as part of the misunderstood youth during the late 1960s. In a way, they conspire with the doctor who sends Susanna to the hospital. Both parties do not seem to understand how she feels.

Other changes are the exclusions of "the other" Lisa, Alice Calais, and Georgina's boyfriend. There is only one boyfriend in the movie, Tobias, Susanna's boyfriend. His character does not appear as such in the book, but is composed out of her boyfriend, her future husband, and details from the episode "Checkmate" (65).

Taken together, the descriptions of characters in the book agree with the cast of the movie. Angelina Jolie as Lisa, for example, appears to be casted and styled as she is described in the book- except for the hair: "Lisa wouldn't be hard to identify. She rarely ate and she never slept, so she was thin and yellow, the way people look when they don't eat, and she had huge bags under her eyes. She had long dark dull hair that she fastened with a silver clip (20)." The yellowish skin and the huge bags under her eyes, all this, we also find in the movie. That she has blonde hair instead of dark hair might have been used to enforce the yellowness. Lisa symbolizes the rebellion against the establishment, she is a girl who could be characterized as belonging to the youth of the late 1960s. She is comparable to R.P. McMurphy in Ken Kesey's One flew over the cuckoo's nest, as she is the one who tries to break the monotony and apathy on the ward. She takes the girls down to the hospital tunnels to play bowling, she breaks into the doctor's office to show them their files, and she is the one who runs away repeatedly. It does not matter that she is always caught after short time, she shows the other girls that her will cannot be broken and, furthermore, that they should be courageous enough to go back to the outer world. And, just like McMurphy, she is the broken hero(ine) at the end.

A striking change from description to cast was made in the case of Valerie, the head nurse. In the book, Susanna describes her as follows: "Valerie was about

thirty. [...] She looked a lot like Lisa, though she was fair.Valerie's hair was beautiful, but she kept it hidden in a braid that she twisted up on the back of her head. [...] Valerie was strict and inflexible and she was the only staff person we trusted (83)." In the movie, Valerie is played by Whoopi Goldberg, so Mangold chooses an African-American woman for the part of the head nurse. This does not seem to be highly realistic when considering the historical context as there were probably not many African-American head nurses to be found in an expensive WASP hospital during the 1960s. The fact that she is the only person who the girls trust, however, is depicted in the close relationship between her and Susanna. Valerie is the one who is decisive for Susanna's recovery, not the therapeutic meetings with Melvin.

The cast of the protagonist is, of course, the most interesting aspect when it comes to evaluating the characters. As she does not describe herself much, the part of Susanna is the one that leaves the most leeway. The only facts we know about her are that she is a sad and directionless 18-year-old girl who wants to become a writer. Winona Ryder fits into the image of a want-to-be writer, and in addition, she has big, melancholic eyes that convey Susanna's sadness as well as they suggest her intellectuality. Her skinny appearance furthermore fits the fragile psyche. As we do not know how Susanna Kaysen looks like in reality, Winona Ryder seems to be the proper cast for the part of the protagonist.

7. Cultural aspects

The 1960s are the cultural and historical background to both the book and the movie. Events like the Vietnam War, and the deaths of Martin Luther King and Robert Kennedy are woven into the plot. "The world didn't stop because we weren't in it anymore; far from it. Night after night tiny bodies fell to the ground on our TV screen: black people, young people, Vietnamese people, poor people-some dead, some only bashed for the moment. [...] Then came the period when people we knew- not knew personally, but knew of- started falling to the ground: Martin Luther King, Robert Kennedy (92)." In the movie, the Vietnam War and Martin Luther King' assassination affect the ward directly: Susanna's boyfriend Tobias is drafted and wants to run away together with her, and the assassination of the civil rights leader deeply affects Valerie, as is shown in a reaction shot of her

where the otherwise tough nurse sadly looks out of the window, smoking a cigarette.

Moreover, the youth movement of that time becomes a topic. For example, the doctor who sends Susanna to McLean thinks she is on drugs, and there is one sequence in the movie where Lisa and Susanna hitchhike with a group of marihuana smoking kids. The girls on the ward are not the type of rebellious young people one imagines when thinking of the hippies, but in one way or another they all rebell against something- and they listen to the music of that time. Susanna rebells against the norms society, which is represented by her parents, wants to impose on her: she decides not to go to college, but to become a writer. Lisa, the sociopath, fights the establishment on the hospital level. She runs away and knows how to circumvent the rules of the hospital, and in this way undermines the authority of the staff.

These aspects can be found in both works. However, in the book, Susanna assimilates herself in the end. Though she becomes a writer and does not get a "proper" job, she has another excuse for getting out: she marries. In the movie, this aspect is changed, maybe because an audience in the late 1990s would not be satisfied with this gender image. In Mangold's movie, Susanna gets out of the hospital through her own effort, and not with the help of a man, that is, through marriage. Thus, she is the young girl who rebells against society and succeeds, whereas in the book, she is somehow defeated by societal norms as she uses them in order to gain her freedom, in order to be able to write. In this respect, the movie depicts her as a much stronger young woman than the book does.

As can be seen from all this, there are a lot of intertextual references, historically and culturally speaking. As already mentioned above, there are also some similarities to Kesey's One flew over the cuckoo's nest. First of all, the story is basically the same, with the difference that Girl, Interrupted takes place on a women's ward. The therapeutical details we get throughout Kaysen's book are similar to those we find in Kesey's, for example, the patients are treated with shocks, they get their medication at regular intervals- even the trade with the pills among the patients can be found in both stories. To some extent, we also find the Big Nurse in Girl, Interrupted: Mrs. McWeeney, the evening nurse. "She had hard gray hair pressed into waves that grasped her scalp like a migraine. The day nurses, following Valerie's lead, wore unbuttoned nurse coats over street clothes.

No such informality with Mrs. McWeeney. She wore a creaky white uniform and spongy ripple-soled nurse shoes that she painted white every week [...] (88)." None of the patients likes this nurse, and the movie takes the similarities to the Big Nurse even further, as her atttitude towards the patients is just like that of Kesey's head nurse. She is friendly, she smiles, but at the same time, she conveys an underlying power that imtimidates the patients on the ward.

8. Concluding remarks

After comparing the book and the movie, one comes to the conclusion that Mangold puts a different thematic emphasis than Kaysen. Technically speaking, we find all the features we also find in the book, that is, the first-person perspective is kept up, expressed by means of subjective camera, voice-over narration, and reaction shots that establish Susanna as the protagonist. But Mangold leaves out most of the philosophical thoughts that play such an important role in the book, and the episodes of the book are transformed into a Hollywood plot which starts out with a dramatic suicide attempt. There are humorous scenes that are meant to evoke sympathy for the mentally ill people, there is an action-movie-showdown that is staged with a lot of jump cuts, and there is a touching ending. In short, the movie contains all important ingredients for a Hollywood movie. In contrast to this stands an unconventional book with a witty and rational first-person narrator, and which is not at all tearjerking.

However, the movie's different emphasis personalizes the rather distanced account Kaysen gives her readers with her book. Furthermore, the cultural background, that is, the historical events we see on the TV screen on the women's ward, and the soundtrack create an atmosphere that takes audience directly back to the 1960s.

The question whether we can believe a crazy person or not is posed in both works. In the book, Susanna gives excerpts out of an encyclopedia, quotes an analyst, and puts documents out of her hospital file into it. In addition, her philosophical thoughts seem logical, and the fact that homosexuality had been considered to be a mental illness for quite some time question the reliability of the doctors rather than her own. In the movie, this aspect is transformed with the help of different camera perspectives and the voice-over. From a subjective camera perspective we get Susanna's personal perception, through reaction shots we get

the objective viewpoint of the events. The occasional shifts in perspective from Susanna to Lisa or Polly support this objectivity.

Though the movie personalizes the events on the ward, it still gives its audience a kind of safety. The movie can be seen as the story of a girl who, back in the 1960s, happened to end up in a mental hospital and got out eventually. The book has the connotation that everybody might go crazy at any time, all of a sudden. "It is easy to slip into a parallel univese. [...] My roommate Georgina came in swiftly and totally, during her junior year at Vassar. She was in a theater watching a movie when a tidal wave of blackness broke over her head. [...] She knew she had gone crazy. (5)."

9. Works cited

Kaysen, Susanna. Girl, Interrupted. London: Virago, 2000.

Lewison, Martin. Plot Summary for Girl, Interrupted. imdb.com (07.08.2002). <us.imdb.com/Plot?0172493>

Girl, Interrupted. Dir. James Mangold. Columbia Pictures, 1999.

CPSIA information can be obtained
at www.ICGtesting.com
Printed in the USA
LVIC080548210512
2841LVUK00001B